W9-CBU-181

MEDIA

➡➡➡ FROM ➡➡➡

NEWS COVERAGE

‹‹ to ››

POLITICAL ADVERTISING

SANDY DONOVAN

LERNER PUBLICATIONS ◆ MINNEAPOLIS

Lerner Publications Comany
A division of Lerner Publishing Group, Inc.
241 First Avenue North
Minneapolis, MN 55401 USA

For reading levels and more information, look up this title at
www.lernerbooks.com.

Main body text set in Calvert MT Std Light 10/16.
Typeface provided by Monotype Typography.

Library of Congress Cataloging-in-Publication Data

Donovan, Sandra, 1967–
      Media : from news coverage to political advertising / by Sandy
Donovan.
            pages cm.— (Inside elections)
        ISBN 978-1-4677-7909-8 (lb : alk. paper) — ISBN 978-1-4677-8525-9
(pb : alk. paper) — ISBN 978-1-4677-8526-6 (eb pdf)
            1. Advertising, Political—United States—Juvenile literature. 2. Mass
media—Political aspects—United States—Juvenile literature. I. Title.
      JK2281.D658 2015
      324.7'30973—dc23   2015000260

Manufactured in the United States of America
1 – VP – 7/15/15

CONTENTS

The ELECTION MEDIA BLITZ

Q uick question: What do memes, video clips, and magazine articles all have in common?

Answer: They're all excellent reasons to put off doing your homework.

OK, you might think so. But they have more than that in common. They're all forms of media. Media includes any means of mass communication, plus the people who produce it.

Media isn't just a way for you to connect with friends or research a school report. It plays a huge role in events that shape our country, including elections. Even if you and your family never follow politics, you've probably been exposed to election coverage through the media. Political ads interrupting your online playlist, jokes on your favorite comedy show, conversations you see on social media—these are among the driving forces of the US political process.

During elections, the media keeps the public informed about candidates and issues. And beyond just reporting events, the media often works to expose problems in an election, from lies told by candidates to faulty voting machines. Meanwhile, candidates and their supporters use media to convince people to vote for them. And the public—including your relatives and neighbors—can use media to join election-related discussions. Those discussions may influence an election's results.

You might hear people complain that media coverage of elections is biased or unfair. You might also hear that certain media outlets are "in the pocket" or "on the payroll" of a political party. And sometimes the media helps spread untrue rumors about candidates.

Still, most election media coverage is protected by the US Constitution's First Amendment, which guarantees people the right to free speech. And many Americans rely on the media to keep them informed and to help them participate in elections.

Understanding media's many roles in elections can help voters sort through the messages they're receiving about candidates. It can also help *you* make sense of the election-related media you come across. Then you can decide what to believe, learn where to find more information, and even figure out how to take part in this slice of American democracy.

Politicians often talk directly to the media. Here, US representative Chaka Fattah of Pennsylvania addresses reporters in 2011.

CHAPTER ONE

REPORTING ELECTION NEWS

All media is not created equal. The YouTube clip from a candidate's speech, the blog post analyzing a campaign promise, the televised interview with a front-runner: these are different forms of media. Technically, media is anything that delivers information—and information is anything you can hear or see. But when we talk about "the media," we generally mean *mass media*—television, printed materials (such as magazines and newspapers), Internet resources (such as blogs, podcasts, and social media), or radio (podcasts for old-school folks).

Those are the main *forms* of media. But there are also different *types* of media. In the United States, media breaks down into three basic types:

Public media is not-for-profit. Its owners don't earn money from it. Instead, public media gets funding from the government, community organizations, or individual supporters (members). In the United States, public media groups include National Public Radio (NPR) and local public radio stations, the Public Broadcasting Service (PBS) and local

Television evening news programs such as *World News Tonight* are well-known sources of election news.

public television channels, and government websites and publications. If you've checked out any of these, you'll know that they feature almost no commercials. Since their operating costs are covered by government funding or other donations and since they don't make extra profits beyond that, they don't need to sell advertising time or space.

Commercial media is for-profit. It tries to earn more money than it spends—usually by charging fees for access or for ads. Commercial media includes most radio stations, network and cable television, newspapers, magazines, and other print publications. These outlets run plenty of ads, including political ads, because advertisers pay for ad slots, boosting the company's profits. A large company may own several commercial media outlets. For instance, a major for-profit news corporation might control a TV network, a radio station, a website, and some social media accounts.

Private media can be for-profit or not-for-profit. It's created and paid for by individuals or groups to spread a specific message, rather than to consider different sides of a story. Election-related private media is usually made by campaigns, political parties, and special interest groups. A political advertisement, a candidate's website and social media accounts, and printed campaign materials such as pamphlets and brochures all count as private media.

During election season, all forms and types of media can inform—and sometimes misinform—the public about candidates and issues. And one way to do that is through news coverage.

Some media outlets cover only major elections—races for the presidency, Congress, or governorships. Other outlets, including certain magazines, news shows, and websites, specifically focus on political news year-round. So election season is the most exciting part of their year. In any case, media outlets that report on the latest election events and the candidates' backgrounds count as part of a specific category of media: the news media. To provide election coverage, most news media outlets work in this way:

- They decide what to cover.
- They collect, analyze, and fact-check information.
- They present the news to the public.

It's a relatively simple process. But it's also a billion-dollar industry. So how exactly does election coverage happen—and how does it shape US elections?

HOW DOES THE MEDIA DECIDE WHAT TO COVER?

If a media outlet decides not to cover a certain topic, the public has fewer opportunities to learn about it. And just imagine how hard it would be to get information if *no* media

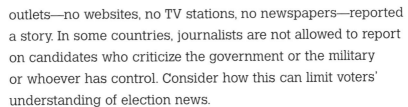

outlets—no websites, no TV stations, no newspapers—reported a story. In some countries, journalists are not allowed to report on candidates who criticize the government or the military or whoever has control. Consider how this can limit voters' understanding of election news.

In the United States, election coverage is more thorough. The US Constitution guarantees the media's right to free speech. But that doesn't mean that all media outlets cover all the news all the time. That's impossible. Even an outlet devoted solely to US election coverage wouldn't be able to capture every election-related development everywhere in the country. So the media has to choose which stories to cover—and which of those stories to spend the most time on.

Those choices largely depend on what a media outlet's audience wants to hear. That's because most media outlets earn profits from ads. Think of the ads you see on websites and in newspapers or the commercials that interrupt online and television programs. An advertiser must pay a website or a station to run those ads. And outlets set their rates based on how many readers or viewers see their ads. So more readers or viewers will mean more income from ads. One way to get a bigger audience, which leads to bigger profits, is to deliver stories that appeal to the audience.

Media outlets do a lot of research to figure out exactly what their audience wants. A few key ideas influence their decisions about what to cover during elections:

- **Audiences love competition.** Think of a sport or a reality show that hooks fans week after week. People are more likely to tune in if there's some suspense about the outcome. For the same reason, the media often focuses on the closest, least predictable elections. And if an election for an important office such as governor or president isn't very competitive, the media tries to gain the public's interest by playing up angles of competition, such as a heated exchange between candidates.

- **Audiences love personalities and personal stories.** Many voters relate more easily to a candidate's personality than to her stance on issues. For instance, the way government collects and uses taxes affects every citizen, but audiences might find that topic dull or confusing. On the other hand, a candidate might adopt a new pet or even get a divorce—neither of which has much to do with governing—and audiences may be fascinated.
- **Many audiences have short attention spans.** Readers, viewers, and listeners may not think they have time to concentrate on campaign issues. So the media tries to hook audiences with quick, exciting stories. It's common for media outlets to present a snapshot of an event, such as a campaign rally or a speech, and offer details about the size and energy of the crowd.

HOW DO JOURNALISTS COLLECT ELECTION INFORMATION?

Once a news media outlet decides what kinds of election stories to cover, journalists collect information for those stories. Most news media outlets also expect their journalists to double-check their facts or at least keep track of different points of view so that they can avoid inaccuracies in their reports. Here are some approaches a journalist might use to prepare a news story:

- **Interviews with candidates.** A formal interview may be a short conversation involving just a few questions and answers. Or it may be a multi-session, in-depth discussion. A journalist usually records an interview

Michigan senator Debbie Stabenow talks with journalists, who record what she says. Most reporters fact-check a politician's statements before publishing them as fact.

so that the candidate's exact words can be used in a news story—or so any summary of the candidate's statements can later be checked against what the candidate actually said.

- **Press conferences.** Candidates and their campaign staffers arrange press conferences to announce important events, such as a decision to run for office, or relatively minor events, such as travel plans. Members of the media attend these events to get firsthand information from candidates.
- **Press releases and other statements.** Candidates, their campaign staff, and political parties frequently release scripted documents detailing a candidate's stance on one or more issues. These documents are generally e-mailed directly to media outlets. Outlets sometimes reprint those press releases word-for-word, and journalists sometimes use them as background information for larger stories.
- **In-depth research.** A journalist can review a

campaign's records to see how much money the campaign has raised and spent or check a candidate's record on important issues. A reporter might also scour old newspapers, magazines, or even high school yearbooks to learn more about a candidate. And it's common for journalists to track down and interview anyone who might know details about a candidate's life or work.

- **Time on the campaign trail.** For major elections, journalists can be assigned to cover one or more candidates for months. These journalists crisscross the country with a candidate's campaign tour, covering voter rallies, attending press conferences, taking photos and video footage, and trying to schedule as many interviews with the candidate as possible.

Most journalists use a mix of these news-gathering approaches, depending on the type of story. For a short piece, a journalist may have just one source, such as a direct quote from a candidate. For longer, more complex stories, journalists might consult several public records and talk to a lot of people, from members of the campaign to a candidate's opponents to experts on an issue.

HOW DO JOURNALISTS PRESENT ELECTION NEWS?

Once journalists have their information, the news media can package that information for audiences in several different ways, from ultra brief to extremely in-depth. Here are some common ways the media presents election news:

- **Sound bites.** These brief one-phrase or simple-sentence quotes can define a candidate's image. A punchy quote sometimes becomes the one thing that voters know about a candidate. Media outlets select

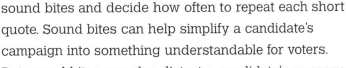

sound bites and decide how often to repeat each short quote. Sound bites can help simplify a candidate's campaign into something understandable for voters. But sound bites can also distort a candidate's message by placing too much focus on a few words. Most sound bites come from much longer speeches or interviews.

The Sting of the Sound Bite

When former Massachusetts governor Mitt Romney challenged Barack Obama for the presidency in 2008, both candidates fielded tough questions under the media spotlight. And both candidates floundered because of sound bites that came back to haunt them.

In a campaign speech, Obama famously said, "If you've got a business, you didn't build that." The rest of his remarks made it clear that he meant small-business owners always have help from others. But the words "You didn't build that" made their way into media coverage and sparked outrage. Republicans claimed Obama had insulted hardworking entrepreneurs.

During a presidential debate, Romney said that he'd worked to increase the number of women on his staff. He spoke of reviewing "binders full of women" in search of qualified job applicants.

Romney's full statement emphasized his commitment to women's equality. But the media latched onto four words: "binders full of women." To Romney's critics, those words showed that he didn't truly respect women or take the issue of workplace equality seriously.

So did either candidate lose votes because of sound bites? Media researchers say probably not. People who were already planning to vote for Romney were happy with his response at the debate, and most people who were offended by the sound bite had already decided not to vote for him. As for Obama, he won reelection despite his sound bite mishap.

Taking a quote out of its original context can change its meaning.

- **Short reports.** A staple of television news and many daily newspapers, the short report usually takes up less than a minute of airtime or a paragraph or two in print. A short report might recap the highlights of a campaign event or announce the results of a new poll—usually the percentage of voters expected to vote for each candidate. The report may include some additional information, but it isn't meant to give a complete view of a candidate or a campaign.

- **In-depth reports.** Longer profiles are found most often in print and online magazines, in major newspapers, and on weekly television news shows. One or more journalists may spend weeks or even months following a candidate on the campaign trail, digging into the candidate's background, and crafting a detailed presentation of the candidate's statements and actions.

- **Analysis.** Extended election news coverage often includes analysis. Instead of reporting only *what* is happening, analysis tackles *how* and *why* it's happening. Say a candidate switches her position on an issue in the middle of her campaign. What are her reasons for doing that? In what ways will it affect her chances in the race? What other events might be triggered by the change? No one in the media knows the answers to these questions. But people with knowledge about the issue, the candidate, and related issues can make educated guesses. That's analysis in a nutshell: an educated guess.

- **Commentary.** Election news coverage isn't just about facts. The news media features plenty of opinions too.

ANALYSIS VS. COMMENTARY

MEDIA FORM	EXAMPLE OF ANALYSIS	EXAMPLE OF COMMENTARY
Television	An expert guest (such as a historian, a professor, or a scientist) on a news program	*The Daily Show with Jon Stewart* (liberal commentary), *The O'Reilly Factor* (conservative commentary)
Print	An article labeled "analysis" in the front section of a newspaper	An editorial written by members of a newspaper's staff
Internet	A blog post by an expert (such as a historian, a professor, or a scientist) on a topic related to his or her expertise	A blog post by a political figure or an activist
Radio	A public affairs program on National Public Radio	*The Rush Limbaugh Show* (conservative commentary), *The Stephanie Miller Show* (liberal commentary)

Expressing an opinion and trying to convince other people of that opinion is called commentary. An author or a speaker explains and defends a particular point of view based on related events, facts, or candidate statements. Some media outlets, such as major newspapers, try to keep commentary separate from fact-focused news coverage and analysis. But other outlets aren't as clear about where factual reporting ends and commentary begins.

BREAKING NEWS: GOOD OR BAD?

Scroll through the news feed feature on a web browser. Most of the stories near the top of the list were probably published within

Journalist Tom Brokaw *(right)* interviewed presidential candidate Barack Obama *(left)* in 2008 for the news show *Meet the Press*.

Yes. Part of the media's mission is to act as an election watchdog—making sure that campaigns are run fairly and truthfully. That means uncovering lies a candidate has told, inconsistencies in a candidate's claims or plans, and facts that a candidate gets wrong. The media is often called the fourth branch of government. Along with the executive, the legislative, and the judicial branches of government, media outlets play a key role in the checks and balances of US democracy.

MEDIA BIAS

To promote fairness in elections, media outlets first have to ensure fairness in their own work. Election coverage often prompts accusations of media bias. That's when a media outlet favors one point of view above another. Bias might show up in the language that journalists use or in the number and type of stories that a media outlet runs. For instance, consider these two sentences:

Governor No-Name faced his attackers head-on with an energetic speech.

Governor No-Name lashed out at his critics today with an aggressive speech.

How does the word choice in each sentence affect the candidate's image? Neither statement is factually incorrect (assuming Governor No-Name did make a speech today). But the first statement puts a positive spin on Governor No-Name's speech, while the second statement makes him sound unpleasant and maybe even out of control.

You might be thinking, *What's the big deal? These are really minor differences.* But tiny cues like this can build up and shape voters' impressions of a candidate or an issue. And plenty of media bias is more extreme. Imagine that Governor No-Name is holding a baby for a photo op and almost drops the baby. Most media outlets run a brief story about this right after it happens. But one outlet keeps talking about the incident for weeks. It replays a video clip of the baby almost being dropped, interviews the baby's relatives, and speculates that Governor No-Name might be just as bad at handling the country's problems as he is at holding a squirming baby. Think about how this kind of coverage can sway voters and distract them from larger issues.

It's nearly impossible for any media outlet to be completely unbiased. If your entire class had to write a report on chipmunks, no report would be exactly the same, even if every report was well-researched and accurate. Each student's ideas of what's most important and interesting about chipmunks would be slightly different.

That happens with every form and type of media. Members of the media have different opinions and different ways of interpreting information. The critical responsibility of media outlets that strive to be balanced is to keep those biases in check—by monitoring both the language they use and the news they choose to report.

Some media outlets choose to deal with bias by admitting it up front rather than trying to rein it in. For instance, a newspaper might publicly endorse, or recommend, a candidate for office. Members of the paper's staff write an editorial

OPPOSING VIEWPOINTS: ON MEDIA BIAS

PRO

"Rather than ripping news outlets for 'slanting' the news . . . I prefer to blame news consumers for journalism's deficiencies: Readers and viewers aren't as critical about their favorite news outlets as they should be. . . . Have readers and viewers expand the range of news sources they consume. . . . Media bias isn't a journalistic problem. It's a solution."
—Jack Shafer, Reuters columnist, September 20, 2011

CON

"[Media bias] can begin to build a view of the world in which any deviation is considered either wrong-headed or purposeful propaganda. . . . Those who hear and read this [view] daily begin to believe anyone questioning any of this is ignorant . . . and perhaps even a bad person."
—Dennis Clayson, Waterloo-Cedar Falls Courier columnist, February 1, 2015

explaining their reasons for throwing the paper's support behind this candidate. Or a website might have a statement of purpose that explains its particular slant on the issues.

Sometimes bias is about a specific issue rather than an overall political view. Suppose that in the lead-up to a small town's school board election, a local newspaper gives extra coverage to a candidate who supports arts programs for local schools. The newspaper may be biased about this issue, but its presentation of other news may be fair and objective.

More often, bias is general. The owners and employees of a media outlet may share an overall political outlook—or at least audiences may think they do. Research shows that in the United States, people who are politically conservative tend to think the news media is liberally biased, meaning that it promotes a liberal viewpoint. People with liberal leanings, on the other hand, tend to think the media is conservatively biased. For instance, Fox News is often labeled as conservatively biased. The *Rachel Maddow Show* on MSNBC is often labeled as liberally biased. Many studies have been

Audience Bias

Regardless of how politically biased major media outlets may be, research shows that voters are biased about which media they follow. One survey found that those identified as "consistently conservative" got their election news from different sources than those identified as "consistently liberal." Nearly half of consistent conservatives (47 percent) said Fox News was their main source of news about politics and government. Consistent liberals identified four main sources for political and government news: CNN (15 percent), National Public Radio (13 percent) MSNBC (12 percent), and the *New York Times* (10 percent).

conducted to determine if various media outlets really are politically biased. One of the largest found that many outlets are conservatively biased, many others are liberally biased, and overall they balance each other out.

THE EQUAL-TIME RULE

One way the media can promote fairness in elections is by giving each candidate an equal chance to reach voters. Imagine if a news media outlet reported only what one candidate says, does, or believes. Voters would have a hard time learning about other candidates. The US government has been concerned about this since at least 1934, when it passed the Communications Act. This law says that any radio or television station that provides airtime to one candidate must also provide an equal opportunity to any opposing candidate who requests it. So if a television station runs a half-hour show on Candidate X, anyone running against Candidate X also has a right to thirty minutes of airtime.

The equal-time rule is still in effect, but the government has added four exceptions. When a candidate is on the air as part of a documentary, a scheduled newscast (such as an evening news show), a news interview, or an on-the-spot news event, equal time is not required. Those exceptions mean that the equal-time rule doesn't apply to most candidate coverage. And the law doesn't cover Internet programs at all.

Few candidates, voters, or media outlets have taken the law very seriously in recent decades. In 2003 *The Tonight Show with Jay Leno* poked fun at the law after Arnold Schwarzenegger, running for governor of California, appeared on the show. Host Jay Leno invited other candidates—eighty of them—to have ten seconds of equal time. He then ran all of their responses at exactly the same time, so television viewers couldn't understand any of them.

THE EQUAL-TIME RULE

PROS:

- The rule discourages media outlets from favoring some candidates over others.

- The rule gives candidates a legal tool to fight media exclusion.

- The rule upholds people's right to free speech.

CONS:

- The rule can't be enforced because with so many media outlets, it's too hard to regulate who gets airtime and who doesn't.

- The rule doesn't legally apply to most modern forms of media.

- No one actually abides by the rule, so few candidates benefit from it.

PROMOTING TRANSPARENCY

Realistically, media outlets can't always cover every angle of an election story or give equal attention to every candidate, just as they can't completely filter bias out of their coverage. But they can do the next best thing: work to ensure transparency in elections. They can provide their audiences with access to publicly available facts and data. Then voters can review the facts and form their own opinions.

Imagine you're doing a school report on a candidate. What kind of information could you find with a quick online search? The candidate's birth date, political party, and terms in public office would be easy. But did you know you can also find out who has donated to that candidate's campaigns and how much money each donor has given? The government requires candidates to report this information. The idea is that voters should know who is investing money in candidates, because candidates tend to share the beliefs and goals of their major supporters. For instance, if an animal rights group gives a lot of money to a candidate for Congress, that candidate might support pro-animal laws if elected.

And did you realize you can access a candidate's entire voting record if the candidate has served in Congress, a state legislature, a city council, or another governing body? An officeholder votes on thousands of bills. Has Candidate Z always voted the same way on certain issues? Do her votes usually match the votes of other politicians in her party? You can check for yourself.

You can even find government reports that analyze laws on taxes, education, or the environment. And you can compare those reports to a candidate's statements. The candidate might explain a law very differently from the experts who put together a report. What might this reveal about the candidate's goals and biases?

All this information is available to the public. But it can be hard to find. It doesn't usually get featured in TV news segments or start trending on Twitter. But many media outlets provide easy access to the information. A newspaper may reprint information from a public record. More often, a fact-checking website will repost documents or statistics for voters to view in full.

KEEPING CANDIDATES ACCOUNTABLE

Ensuring transparency in elections is a major way for the media to fulfill its watchdog duties. But making records available is one thing. Actually keeping candidates accountable for their words and actions is a tougher job.

Candidates and their supporters make a lot of statements during a campaign. Sometimes somebody gets the facts wrong by accident. Other times, people make false claims on purpose. The news media is responsible for finding and reporting the truth.

The first step is to ask candidates questions directly. Journalists have a chance to do this at press conferences and during one-on-one interviews. It might mean asking questions about specific issues, even if the candidates seem to want to talk about something else. A reporter has the right to ask a question and then report that the candidate refused to answer it or that the candidate responded but didn't provide a real answer. Reporters can also ask follow-up questions, pushing candidates to clear up misleading or vague statements.

Beyond talking to the candidates, journalists can research facts and figures. For instance, if a candidate for reelection says that she has never voted to raise taxes, a journalist can request and review her voting records to check. Or if a candidate says that his campaign has never taken money from a special interest group, a journalist can request the candidate's campaign finance records to see if that's true. When candidates make claims about how their proposed policies will affect citizens, journalists can talk to experts to learn if those statements are accurate.

Journalists can also talk to additional sources to check that a candidate's story matches other people's recollections or documentation. Media members might contact a candidate's former neighbors, family members, coworkers, and campaign staff—and even the staff of an opposing campaign. Even if a media outlet can't say for sure who's right, it can at least report the various points of view.

So does all this work make a difference? That depends. Some politicians may be more careful about their statements if they think the media will catch a lie or a mistake. But others won't change their ways. They may think that the media won't be able to prove them wrong, either because the facts aren't publicly available or because journalists won't know

A key part of a journalist's job is to research and verify the facts of her story.

where to look. Or candidates may feel that even if the media eventually exposes a lie, plenty of voters will still believe that lie. One of Vice President George H. W. Bush's staffers made this point in 1984. When the press followed up on an inaccurate statement Bush had made during the vice presidential debate, his press secretary, Peter Teeley, said, "You can say anything you want during a debate, and 80 million people hear it." He added that it didn't matter much whether the media later corrected it. "So what," he said. "Maybe 200 people read [the correction] or 2,000 or 20,000."

In many cases, Teeley's opinion may still hold true. Even if the media calls out or corrects a candidate's false statement, that might not be enough to set the record straight for voters. The original message may reach and influence more people than the correction does. Once voters have heard something they find believable, it tends to stick in their minds. They're less likely to accept new information if it contradicts what they already believe.

Yet many people support the media's watchdog role and believe it works. A 2013 study showed that a majority of people in the United States—68 percent—believe the eagle eyes of the media have a positive impact on politicians' behavior. And about half—48 percent—say the media helps protect democracy.

CHAPTER THREE

CANDIDATES and MEDIA RELATIONS

During elections, journalists and other media staff uncover most of their information directly, through interviewing and researching. But candidates and their campaign staff also play a big role in getting information to the media. All but the smallest campaigns have media relations staff. It's their job to get the candidate's message in front of voters. To achieve this goal, campaign staffers come up with a media relations plan, a strategy for how to interact with media outlets and journalists. This plan involves several steps:

- Building good relationships with members of the media
- Framing the candidate's message for media coverage
- Helping the candidate present the best image
- Staging special events designed to help boost the candidate's profile in the media

BUILDING TRUST WITH THE MEDIA

Gaining journalists' trust and respect is a big part of a campaign media staffer's job. Generally, just a few journalists per media outlet are assigned to cover a candidate. A local

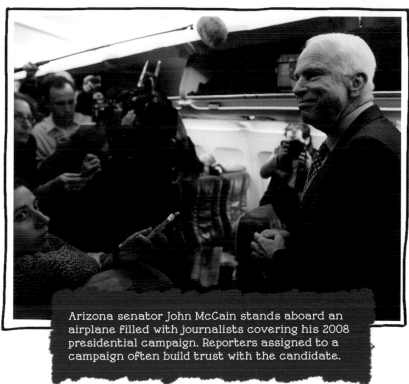

Arizona senator John McCain stands aboard an airplane filled with journalists covering his 2008 presidential campaign. Reporters assigned to a campaign often build trust with the candidate.

election might involve only a handful of local outlets: a local newspaper, a television station, and a radio station, for example. But for a huge national election, hundreds of media outlets could be interested, so campaign staffers have many more journalists to get to know.

Whatever the size of the election, campaign staffers try to learn the names and backgrounds of journalists assigned to cover their candidate. Then they make the most of the methods journalists use to collect information. They know whom to send press releases to and whom to follow up with. They know whom to reach out to when they schedule an event or want to set up an interview. When staffers have earned a journalist's goodwill, the journalist is more likely to run their press releases, schedule interviews, or even return their phone calls.

Media staffers try to build a comfortable—but not too personal—relationship with those reporters. Staffers want journalists to feel close enough to the campaign to present the candidate to audiences. But staffers know that responsible journalists don't want the relationship to become *too* close. If journalists get overly friendly with campaign staffers, they risk becoming biased about the candidate. And some candidates may have secrets that campaigns don't want journalists to discover. Those secrets might be strategies for winning the election, which the candidate doesn't want her opponents to hear about on the news. Or they could be more damaging secrets: problems in the candidate's personal life, plans to break a campaign promise, or even shady business deals. Sometimes campaigns have as much to hide as they have to share. So staffers try to win media members' trust without giving the media too much access.

FRAMING CANDIDATES' MESSAGES FOR THE MEDIA

Campaign staffers want to get their candidate's name mentioned in the media as much as possible. People aren't likely to vote for someone they haven't heard about. So, especially in smaller elections, just getting a candidate's name in print, on air, or online can boost a candidate's chances.

But that's easier said than done. Major media outlets get swamped with campaign materials during election season. Most journalists won't use a story unless it strikes them as especially important or exciting. So to actually get coverage, a campaign needs to provide the attention-grabbing stories or memorable quotes that the media is looking for.

Part of the secret is timing. Candidates often comment on other events that are big in the news. If the media is already covering an incident, a candidate's statement about it will fit

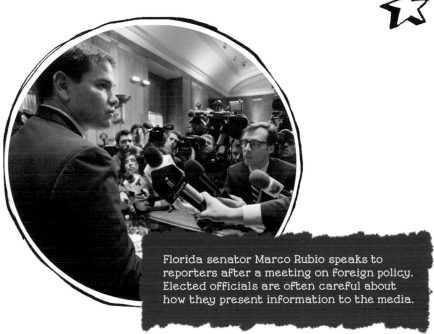

Florida senator Marco Rubio speaks to reporters after a meeting on foreign policy. Elected officials are often careful about how they present information to the media.

in well with the larger story. And candidates can use current events to draw attention to their wider messages. Suppose a major hurricane is sweeping through several US states. A candidate might use this as a chance to talk about his plans for disaster response or even to unveil a new environmental policy idea. On the flip side, on a slow news day, a fairly dull announcement from a campaign might get more coverage than it would in the middle of a national emergency. And a presidential candidate's visit to Iowa would be big news before the Iowa primary—but *after* the Iowa primary, not so much. Campaigns try to time most speeches and activities so that they seem newsworthy.

And campaigns aren't just careful about *when* they release information to the media. They also put a lot of work into *how* the message is expressed. Consider sound bites. Campaigns can't control which quotes from their candidates will be picked up by the media—or can they? Many candidates' speeches are designed to include prime sound bite material: short, punchy lines that grab people's attention. If a candidate

Minnesota senator Al Franken eats lunch with elementary school students. Soon after the media covered this event, Franken introduced a bill addressing reduced-price school lunches.

repeats a slogan or a catchphrase enough, it's likely to get media coverage. Campaign speech writers try to craft witty, forceful, or touching one-liners for their candidates. And media relations staffers feed those messages to journalists at every opportunity.

ALL ABOUT IMAGE

You might hear the expression "Any press is good press," but as much as possible, campaign staffers want their candidates to appear in a favorable light. So they work to increase the number of positive stories and decrease negative coverage about their candidate. That has a lot to do with packaging the candidate's message. But it's also about making the candidate seem likable. Research shows that voters are most likely to vote for candidates they relate to and like on a personal level.

So campaigns try to organize activities that will make the candidate seem appealing. Visits to schools, community centers, restaurants, and businesses are always staged with media coverage in mind. Do voters view a candidate as too stiff and formal? Her campaign may respond with a photo op of the candidate sipping a milk shake while playing with her dog. Are a candidate's supporters worried that he isn't as young or healthy as his opponent? Don't be surprised when his skydiving trip makes headlines.

SPECIAL EVENTS

Much of the relationship building between campaigns and the media happens during the ongoing activities of the campaign. But sometimes special events are scheduled, such as press conferences and hosted debates.

A campaign might schedule a press conference for a few reasons:

- To announce an important development and give a candidate a chance to answer follow-up questions or emphasize specific points
- To increase a candidate's chances of appearing on television, because press conferences provide ready-made news stories
- To set the record straight if a candidate has gotten negative publicity

Campaign staff arrange the time and the location for a press conference and then invite members of the media to attend. Staffers usually send out a packet, called a press kit, that provides journalists with extra information. This increases the chance that the media will present the topic in the way the candidate wants. The press kit might contain the names and short biographies of participants, a press release with a topic summary and a few quotes, background information and statistics about the issue, and even photographs. Think of the press kit as the teaser trailer for the press conference. It's

A DELICATE BALANCE

For campaign staff, the news media is both a tool and a threat. It can be a helpful tool for spreading a candidate's message and crafting a candidate's public image. But media outlets can also pounce on any lie, mistake, or awkward moment that slips into a candidate's campaign. A flubbed line at a press conference can be posted and reposted online, to be rewatched and analyzed by media members and the general public. A photo of a candidate's tacky tie can go from a journalist's phone to her Instagram account in seconds, and that image can turn into a viral meme in minutes.

What voters remember about a debate, a press conference, or a moment on the campaign trail may largely come down to what the media says about it afterward. Which clips get replayed and reposted most? Which talking points get the most attention from respected media analysts? Which

Incumbent Barack Obama (right) debates Mitt Romney (center) in 2012. Televised debates give voters at home an opportunity to see and hear the candidates speak about important issues.

Did You Watch the Debate? What about *SNL*?

Journalist and newscaster Gwen Ifill, who moderated vice presidential debates in 2004 and 2008, credits the sketch comedy show *Saturday Night Live* with influencing voters' opinions far more than actual debates. *SNL* jokingly reenacts presidential and vice presidential debates, with actors and comedians playing the candidates. As Ifill puts it, "Whether it's Tina Fey as [Sarah] Palin, Amy Poehler as Hillary Rodham Clinton or Jason Sudeikis as [Mitt] Romney or Vice President Biden, a dead-on impersonation that lampoons a candidate's most cartoonish qualities can leave a nasty mark."

statements and gestures are parodied on comedy shows? Campaign staffers are constantly thinking about how to present their candidate to the media—while the media decides how to present their candidate to the world.

CHAPTER FOUR

PRIVATE POLITICAL MEDIA

Building relationships with media outlets is one way candidates try to use the news media to their advantage. But these relationships only go so far. Candidates and their supporters don't have the final say over how the news media presents them or even which of their quotes become sound bites. So candidates, their campaigns, and the special interest groups connected to them often use private media to shape their messages and images. From printed brochures to campaign websites to political ads, private political media can paint a very different picture of an election than you'll find in the news media.

CONNECTING DIRECTLY WITH VOTERS

Candidates have always spent a lot of time meeting people face-to-face in the hope of making a good impression and gaining more votes. But campaigns also use social media to interact directly with voters the candidates may never meet.

Barack Obama was one of the first major office seekers to create a strong social media presence. When he first ran for president in 2008, he connected with millions of voters through Facebook, Twitter, and YouTube, as well as his official campaign website. Experts believed his success with social media helped him win the election.

Since that breakthrough, campaigns usually set up their own websites and social media accounts. Major campaigns have Facebook and Twitter accounts that allow voters to interact with candidates directly. Some campaigns set up accounts on various other platforms as well. Campaigns use these accounts to tell voters where candidates stand on issues, who's supporting them, where and when they are scheduled to appear, and how supporters can donate. Voters can comment, like, and share with their own social media contacts.

Online Donations

Raising money is one of the most important tasks of candidates and their campaigns. And social media and the Internet have changed fund-raising just as much as they've changed the shape of public discussions.

Campaigns used to send out mail or knock on people's doors to raise money. Those methods can be expensive and time-consuming. But online, campaigns can reach more potential donors more easily and cheaply. They can send mass e-mail requests for donations, plus follow-up e-mails reminding supporters of the deadline and saying how much money they still need to meet their goals. Appeals on social media can help prod supporters as well. And donors can give money in just a few clicks. In 2007 candidate Ron Paul raised $4 million online in one day. And in both 2008 and 2012, Barack Obama raised hundreds of millions from small donations online.

More and more, candidates are using social media to connect directly with voters. One study found that the number of Americans who follow political figures on social media grew from 6 percent of all voters in 2010 to 16 percent in 2014. Many of these users feel more personally connected to the political candidates or groups they follow, and they believe they can get faster, more reliable information via a candidate's social media presence than through traditional news organizations.

CAMPAIGN ADS

During election season, paid political ads flood television screens, radio waves, newspapers, and the Internet. Even programs and websites that have nothing to do with politics or news might run political ads. Remember that for-profit companies make much of their money by selling advertising slots. And political ads are a huge business. Of the billions of dollars spent by candidates, parties, and other groups in national elections, most goes to television advertising.

If you've watched any TV or spent time online during election season, you've probably seen or heard a political ad. It might have been a video, an audio clip, or a web banner ad. Video or audio ads are usually less than a minute long, and banner ads include only a few lines of text. But these are meant to be memorable snapshots of a candidate or of an issue. The goal of a political ad is to catch voters' attention and win their support with a few carefully chosen details. Ads can include short blurbs about where candidates stand on certain issues. They can also list a candidate's endorsements—recommendations by prominent groups or people—to show voters who else supports the candidate.

Political ads have a bad reputation in the United States. Many of the ads are negative, focusing on opponents' flaws

These ads focus their messages on attacking their opponents. Would either of these ads inspire you to vote Democrat or Republican?

instead of candidates' strengths. Some ads make claims that aren't true. And voters complain that there are simply too many ads in the months and even years before an important election. Often, though, candidates use ads to responsibly spread their message to voters. Ads can be especially helpful for candidates running in smaller, local elections, which may receive less media coverage.

ATTACK ADS

European countries ban political advertising on television. Instead of letting candidates and political parties buy television time to run ads, many of those countries provide set amounts of free on-air time to each candidate. And many have rules about what can or can't be said during that time. For instance, in France, candidates aren't allowed to criticize their opponents.

In the United States, that's not the case. In fact, a lot of ads are extremely negative. Negative ads are often called attack ads. Some criticize an opponent's voting record or the opponent's stance on a particular issue. Many use an opponent's sound bites—sometimes out of context—to make a point about the candidate's beliefs.

Public opinion polls show that these aren't the types of negative ads voters dislike most. Harsher styles are much more unpopular with the public. These ads sometimes call an opponent's personal character into question. For instance, when former House Speaker Newt Gingrich ran for the 2012 Republican Party presidential nomination, ads by his opponents criticized the fact that he had been married three times. Other attack ads play into voters' fears without using facts for support. These ads try to convince voters that the world will be worse off if an opponent is elected.

Most Americans believe negative ads have gotten worse over the last twenty years, but attack ads are nothing new. The first famous attack ad aired in 1964 in support of Democrat Lyndon B. Johnson's presidential campaign. The ad shows a young girl picking petals off a daisy. The camera zooms in on her face as a voice-over begins a countdown followed by a nuclear explosion. The ad never mentions Johnson's opponent, but it implies that he will lead the country into nuclear war. A final voice-over says, "We must either love each other or we must die . . . vote for President Johnson on November 3. The stakes are too high for you to stay home."

Still, candidates have one big reason for holding back in their attack ads: their names are on them. Any candidate running for federal office is required by law to take responsibility for television or radio ads made by the candidate's campaign—or made by supporters with the candidate's permission.

ATTACK ADS

PROS:

- They're an exercise of free speech guaranteed by the Constitution.

- Attack ads provide information to voters who wouldn't otherwise be exposed to it.

- Unlike positive ads, they encourage voters to question their leaders and those running for office.

CONS:

- Wealthy individuals and groups can afford to pay for more attack ads than other groups, drowning out opposing voices.

- They create negative feelings about politics and the democratic process, which discourages some people from being more engaged in political discussion.

- They often deliberately mislead voters.

You frequently hear "I'm [candidate's name] and I approve this message." Most candidates don't want to be associated with messages that make them look mean.

But what about attack ads made by special interest groups instead of candidates themselves? Most of these ads don't have the same restrictions because they're not directly tied to any candidate. Special interest groups that make ads have to state their names in those ads, but they don't have to state which candidate they're supporting. Many special interest groups choose vague names too. No wonder voters are often unaware of who's really behind the ads. They only see and remember the negative messages.

Private political media can rub many voters the wrong way. But it also has a strong influence over public opinion. And because so many Americans distrust the news media to some extent, campaigns have a chance to gain loyal followers by creating convincing media messages of their own.

The Attack Ad Blitz of 2014

The 2014 election season added plenty of attack ads to the airwaves. In Texas the Democratic candidate for governor, Wendy Davis, ran an especially controversial ad. It featured a photo of an empty wheelchair while a voice-over discussed her opponent, Greg Abbott, who uses a wheelchair. The ad went viral on YouTube and sparked intense criticism.

While many thought Davis's ad was overly personal, other ads took flak for being factually incorrect. An ad supporting David Perdue, Georgia's Republican candidate for the US Senate, for example, claimed that his Democratic opponent, Michelle Nunn, "funded organizations linked to terrorists." But numerous fact-checking websites disproved the claim within days of the ad's first appearance.

CHAPTER FIVE

PROMOTING PUBLIC DISCUSSION

Media coverage in the United States isn't just a one-way street. Beyond simply delivering information, media gives everyone a chance to participate in public discussions. During election season, those discussions often focus on candidates, issues, and races. People write letters to the editor of newspapers, call in to radio talk shows, and share and comment on news online.

For many people, the ability to engage in public discussion is just as important as casting a vote. It's a key part of US democracy. Through media, consumers can share opinions, experiences, and information—true or not—related to candidates. They debate the issues, how they think the election is going, and even the quality of media coverage.

ONLINE CONVERSATIONS

Around the United States, print newspapers continue to receive traditional letters to the editor. Many readers compose formal letters and mail or e-mail them to a newspaper. After receiving a letter, the paper may take a day or more to decide

Anyone with access to the Internet can comment on election news and join online conversations about political races.

whether to print it. Once a letter gets printed, other letter writers may respond and start a public discussion. That discussion takes shape over several days or weeks.

The Internet provides a much faster channel for public discussion. After finding a news article online, a person can immediately post a public comment. And others may post responses within minutes or even seconds. The discussion is immediate—and it can involve many more people than would have taken part in a traditional letter-to-the-editor exchange.

It can also be anonymous, since people don't have to use their real names when commenting on a public article. So if they post incorrect information or even if they insult others, they face few consequences. Some forums can ban users who are extremely abusive. But consider any YouTube clip of a campaign speech or any online article about an upcoming election. Plenty of the comments are rude, not to mention inaccurate. So voters who turn to Internet discussions have to sort through a lot of material and think carefully about what to believe.

Online newspapers and magazines, along with news websites, are popular spaces for public discussions of election issues. But increasingly those discussions also occur on social media, where content comes from users instead of professional media writers. In 2014 Facebook created an elections dashboard to make it easier for Facebook users to interact about election issues. Twitter also introduced an

OPPOSING VIEWPOINTS: ON SOCIAL MEDIA AND POLITICAL NEWS COVERAGE

"At the height of the campaign season . . . most social media users . . . are using the tools to debate others, stay in touch with candidates, flag political news stories and analysis that are important to them, and press their friends into action. We'll see the fruits of this neo-activism on Election Day."
—Lee Rainie, Pew Internet Project director, October 2012

PRO

"Facebook is allowing us to crowdsource reality. If we think it's true, it stands. If we think it's false, down it goes. . . . We are the tailors of our own realities, and we proudly wear what we stitch. At least until someone comes along and points out that . . . we're not wearing much at all."
—Rex Huppke, Chicago Tribune columnist, January 27, 2015

CON

elections page with data on who's tweeting what, as well as which election issues are getting the most tweets.

Posting on social media and commenting on others' posts is a fast and simple way to expand election discussions. Of course, it's also a fast and simple way for the discussion to turn ugly. When people can instantly post their opinions without seeing their fellow commenters face-to-face, they're more likely to make unkind or untrue statements about candidates and their supporters.

Many people create blogs as another quick and easy way to communicate their opinions about candidates and issues in elections. Blogs are more formal than a lot of social media platforms, since you have to set up your own official blogging site. But that's still much simpler than launching a full website or online journal. People can also record themselves discussing an issue and upload the footage to YouTube or other sites. These public media forums encourage comments, which keep the conversation rolling.

SHARING THE SCOOP

Thanks to online consumers, election news from one media outlet doesn't stay on that media outlet. People can repost or link to news articles, pictures, videos, cartoons, memes, or any other kind of election-related communication. "Sharing" instantly multiplies the number of people who see a story. Consumers can also alter images and sound bites to create new spins on a piece of election news. Think of memes and video remixes that emphasize a candidate's statements, attitudes, or facial expressions. These started out as fragments of other media coverage, but in the hands of the public, they turn into commentary. That commentary can be aimed at the candidate, at a larger issue, or even at the major media outlets covering the election.

SOCIAL MEDIA'S ROLE IN ELECTION DISCUSSIONS

PROS:

- Social media allows anyone who's interested in an election to express opinions and share information, both of which are important ways of participating in a democracy.

- Social media allows people to choose from a variety of platforms and outlets that let them follow and participate in election developments.

- It's faster and simpler for the public to engage in discussion about elections via social media than by interacting through traditional media outlets.

CONS:

- Social media users are more likely to be biased, inaccurate, or deliberately deceptive than professionally trained news reporters.

- The amount of information and discussion on social media is overwhelming. It's impossible to keep track of or engage with it in a meaningful way.

- It's difficult to keep discussions on topic or to keep an in-depth exchange going on social media because so much is happening so quickly.

Sometimes an election-related story, video clip, or image can get so popular that its own popularity becomes news. During the 2012 election season, for instance, media outlets regularly featured roundups of the most popular political memes, most of which poked fun at either Barack Obama or Mitt Romney. And once an article or a piece of commentary starts trending on social media or shows up on a website's "most popular" list, it reaches even more people.

Whether it's produced by major media outlets or created by the public, media keeps the public engaged in elections. As it finds its way to a growing audience, this media can reflect people's feelings about an upcoming election and even help change some voters' minds.

CHANGING WAYS

For hundreds of years, US citizens have participated in public discussions about elections. First, they wrote to newspapers. Later, they could call in to radio and television shows. Since the late 1990s, the Internet has created more and more ways for people to engage with one another and with candidates. Media continues to change, and people continue to find new ways to use it. But whether they're tweeting about candidates or submitting letters to the editor, voters can use media to become deeply involved in the election process.

> CHAPTER SIX

KEEPING ELECTIONS RUNNING SMOOTHLY

Most media coverage of elections has to do with candidates and campaigns. But keeping the public informed about the election process itself is just as important. At the end of the campaign trail, voters actually choose the winners. The media can tell people when, how, and where to vote. Media outlets also report activities at voting sites. And of course, they report the results when the election is over.

THE WHEN, HOW, AND WHERE

Learning about candidates and understanding the issues is important for voters, but so is knowing the most basic Election Day information: Are you eligible to vote? Where do you vote? What time do the polls open and close? Do you need to bring anything with you to vote?

Voters need this information ahead of time, and many media outlets present the answers. However, those answers differ by state, by community, and even by person, so national news outlets can't fill in all the blanks. Local newspapers, television, radio stations, and websites often feature how-to-vote stories in the weeks and even months before an election. They might include any of these resources:

- Voter guides with basic information about races and candidates
- Registration information and deadlines
- Dates for early voting or absentee voting
- Polling place hours and locations—or online search tools that let voters find their polling places by entering their home addresses

On Election Day, most news media outlets highlight the election. This coverage may include more how-to-vote information. Or it might simply encourage audiences to head to the polls, as the *Des Moines Register* did on November 4, 2014, when it declared: "Make History Today: Vote."

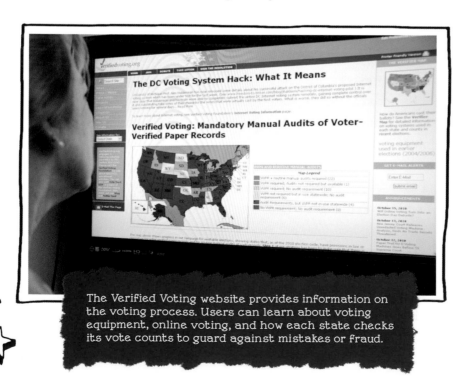

The Verified Voting website provides information on the voting process. Users can learn about voting equipment, online voting, and how each state checks its vote counts to guard against mistakes or fraud.

ELECTION NIGHT COVERAGE

For the media, Election Day can be a whole lot of hurry-up-and-wait. Outlets have been reporting on the candidates and the issues for months. Many have released Election Day guides. And as millions of voters file into their polling places, journalists are preparing for the hours after the polls close. They can't announce election results before that.

Media outlets and journalists still have plenty of work to do throughout Election Day, though. One big job during major elections is exit polling. This is a joint project by a group of media outlets called the National Election Pool. The pool includes NBC, CBS, ABC, Fox, CNN, and the Associated Press (AP)—an organization that includes newspaper, radio, and television reporters. This pool hires an outside company to conduct interviews with voters around the country. Exit poll interviewers ask a certain number of people who have just voted to fill out a written survey. The survey asks voters to record their gender, age, ethnicity, and religion, plus who they voted for. It may also ask a few questions about the major issues.

Having that information helps the media analyze voting results once the election's over. Poll results describe which candidates had the most support from people of certain ages, backgrounds, and genders. And they also help media analysts understand which issues drove voters' decisions. None of that information is available from actual voting records, so the exit polls are a valuable resource for the media.

Polling data can also help the media expose election fraud. If exit polls indicate that Candidate W will win by a landslide, but vote totals say that Candidate Y is the winner, something might be fishy. Someone might have tampered with voting equipment or damaged ballots after they were cast so that they couldn't be counted. Comparing exit polls to official vote tallies is one way the media can detect foul play and call it out to public officials.

The main purpose of exit polls is more immediate and dramatic. They allow the participating media outlets to predict who has won races as soon as possible—just not too soon. News networks aren't supposed to report data that could influence voters to stay home. For instance, in 1980, a television network used exit poll results from the East Coast to predict that Ronald Reagan would win the presidential election. But polling places on the West Coast were still three hours away from closing. Some analysts thought that many West Coast voters decided not to vote after hearing that news.

To avoid situations like that, media outlets wait until all polling places have closed before they announce exit poll results. In some countries, such as the United Kingdom, it's illegal for the media to report exit poll results before voting ends. In the United States, it's legal, but the National Election Pool members agree to a schedule among themselves.

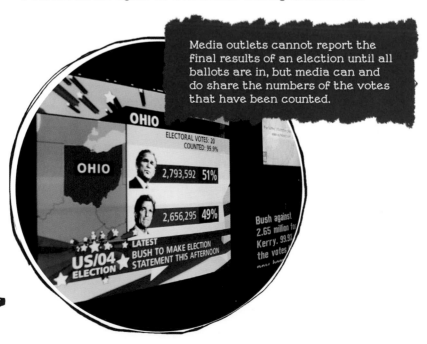

Media outlets cannot report the final results of an election until all ballots are in, but media can and do share the numbers of the votes that have been counted.

OHIO

ELECTORAL VOTES: 20
COUNTED: 99.9%

OHIO

2,793,592 51%

2,656,295 49%

Bush against
2.65 million for
Kerry. 99.9%
the votes,

LATEST
BUSH TO MAKE ELECTION
US/04 STATEMENT THIS AFTERNOON
ELECTION

Breaking the Exit Poll Rules?

After the 2014 midterm congressional elections, the political news website Vox accused Fox News of breaking the rules for exit poll reporting. Fox News anchor Martha MacCallum had discussed exit poll data about New Hampshire's close Senate race nearly two hours before the state's polls closed. MacCallum emphasized that Republican candidate Scott Brown needed support from independent voters—voters who don't identify themselves as either Republicans or Democrats. Her report noted that, according to exit polls, just slightly more independent voters were casting ballots for Brown than for his Democratic opponent, Jeanne Shaheen. Vox claimed this coverage could have discouraged other voters from heading to the polls by making it sound as if Brown was going to win. Fox denied that MacCallum had reported the poll results inappropriately. Shaheen defeated Brown with 51 percent of the vote.

Outlets begin at around five in the afternoon, eastern time, by releasing information about who (in terms of age, race, gender, or political party) has turned out to vote so far. Then, once an area's polls close—about seven in the evening local time—the media can use exit polls to project, or guess, who's going to win in that area.

Meanwhile, media staffers are at election centers as the votes are counted and recorded. These reporters call in the results to news teams, who report those results on air, online, and in print. For a presidential election, television news programs display digital maps of the United States, which are updated each time an entire state's results are known.

EXIT POLLS AS MEDIA TOOLS

PROS:

- Exit polls help the media analyze voting results to predict the election's outcome and keep voters better informed.

- Exit polls help inform political figures about public opinion.

- Exit polls can help uncover fraud, because if an exit poll is very different from actual results, authorities can investigate to find out why.

CONS:

- If exit poll results are released too early, they may discourage people from voting.

- Summarizing the types of people who voted for certain candidates can be a form of stereotyping—and can unnecessarily influence political figures.

- Pollsters sometimes adjust their exit poll data to match the official ballot tally after the polls close, which makes it harder to detect fraud.

REPORTING PROBLEMS AT THE POLLS

In a national election, with thousands of polling places across the country, voting doesn't always go smoothly at every location. Even a minor local election can run into trouble. All sorts of problems can arise: long lines that force people to wait for hours to cast their ballots, glitches with voting equipment, and disturbances near the polls, to name a few. Media outlets look for these hiccups in the voting process, partly because of their watchdog role and partly to better analyze the reasons behind the election results.

These disruptions can make voting difficult for some people and even shift the election's outcome if enough voters give up and go home. Even small inconveniences might be evidence of larger problems. For instance, a broken electronic voting machine might be a fluke—or it might reveal a design flaw that affects other machines too. And protests outside a polling

Long Lines = Big Problems = Big News

In 2012, media outlets around the country reported that thousands of people waited in line for more than five hours to vote in the national election. More than two hundred thousand Florida residents later said they'd eventually just given up and left the polls without casting ballots. The media highlighted similar situations in other states. Spurred by the coverage of these events, President Barack Obama put together a team of experts to study problems in the 2012 election and to come up with ways to make the voting process smoother.

place may point to a broader mood about the election, which media members may want to capture.

THE WHOLE PACKAGE

Election Day wraps up weeks, months, and sometimes years of election coverage. But at every step of the election process, the media plays crucial roles. Media outlets serve as vehicles for candidates and supporters to get their messages out. And they act as voters' main sources of information about the candidates, the issues, and voting. Media makes it possible for voters to sift through the competing statements, opinions, accusations, and other communications that accompany elections. In all, the US media doesn't simply report on elections—it helps them run smoothly, remain fair, and contribute to democracy.

SOURCE NOTES

13 Louis Jacobson, "In Context: Obama's 'You Didn't Build That' Comment," *Tampa Bay Times,* July 18, 2012, http://www.politifact.com/truth-o-meter /article/2012/jul/18/context-obamas-you-didnt-build-comment.

13 Maria Cardona, "Romney's Empty 'Binders Full of Women,'" *CNN,* October 18, 2012, http://www.cnn.com/2012/10/17/opinion/cardona-binders -women/.

27 Paul Waldman, "Mega-Blitz of Ad Spending Makes It Easier for Candidates to Lie," *Washington Post,* October 16, 2014. http://www.washingtonpost .com/blogs/plum-line/wp/2014/10/16/mega-blitz-of-ad-spending-makes -it-easier-for-candidates-to-lie.

20 Jack Shafer, "Media Bias? Give Me More, Please!" Reuters, September 20, 2011, http://blogs.reuters.com/jackshafer/2011/09/20/media-bias-give -me-more-please.

20 Dennis Clayson, "Media Bias Slants News on Climate," *Waterloo-Cedar Falls Courier,* February 1, 2015, http://wcfcourier.com/news/opinion /columnists/media-bias-slants-news-on-climate/article_b7dd4b5d-85b9 -5bfb-9d4a-94373b8f141b.html.

37 Gwen Ifill, "Gwen Ifill Debunks Five Myths about Presidential Debates," Washington Post, September 28, 2012, http://www.washingtonpost.com /opinions/gwen-ifill-debunks-five-myths-about-presidential-debates/2012 /09/28/3eb71112-067f-11e2-858a-5311df86ab04_story.html.

42 Chad Merda, "50 Years Ago, 'Daisy' Set Stage with First Political Attack Ad," *Chicago Sun-Times,* September 8, 2014, http://politics.suntimes.com /article/washington/50-years-ago-daisy-set-stage-first-political-attack-ad /mon-09082014-1133am.

47 Alex Kantrowitz, "Pew: Almost 40% of American Adults Using Social Media for Politics," *Forbes,* October 19, 2012, http://www.forbes.com /sites/alexkantrowitz/2012/10/19/pew-almost-40-of-american-adults -using-social-media-for-politics.

47 Rex Huppke, "True or False? Now We Can Just Vote on It," *Chicago Tribune,* January 27, 2015, http://www.chicagotribune.com/news/opinion /huppke/ct-facebook-hoaxes-huppke-met-20150126-story.html.

52 "Make History Today: Vote," headline, *Des Moines Register,* November 4, 2014, http://www.poynter.org/wp-content/uploads/2014/11/IA_DR.jpg.

GLOSSARY

absentee voting: the formal system allowing voters to send in their vote instead of voting in person on Election Day

analysis: an expert's fact-based interpretation of events or issues

bias: a preference for or dislike of a person, a group, or an idea

blog: a website made up of separate entries called posts that are displayed in reverse chronological order

campaign: the series of activities organized by a candidate for office, aimed at winning an election

commercial: done for profit

conservative: describes a political movement that favors small government and generally does not like radical changes

early voting: the process by which voters can vote before an election. Early voting can take place by mail or in person but usually happens at polling places.

endorsement: a formal recommendation of a candidate by an individual or a group

liberal: describes a political movement that favors reform and broad changes to current systems

mass media: forms of communication with the ability to reach many people at once

media outlet: a publication or a broadcast company that provides news and feature stories to the public

moderator: a person who leads a discussion and tells each person when to speak

nomination: when a political party officially selects a candidate to run for election

platform: technology that allows the creation of Internet-based programs (such as social media)

polling place: a building where voting takes place during an election

primary election: a first election held to narrow the field of candidates for a general election

special interest group: a group of people or an organization that works toward a specific goal

SELECTED BIBLIOGRAPHY

"Amid Criticism, Support for Media's 'Watchdog' Role Stands Out." Pew Research Center. August 8, 2013. http://www.people-press.org/2013 /08/08/amid-criticism-support-for-medias-watchdog-role-stands-out/.

Arnold, R. Douglas. *Congress, the Press, and Political Accountability.* Princeton, NJ: Princeton University Press, 2004.

Black, Eric. "Do Attack Ads Have to Dominate Campaign Season? They Don't in Other Democracies." *MinnPost*, October 20, 2014. http://www.minnpost .com/eric-black-ink/2014/10/do-attack-ads-have-dominate-campaign -season-they-dont-other-democracies.

Harms, William. "For Presidential Candidates, Image May Trump Debate Issues." *UChicago News,* October 24, 2012. http://news.uchicago.edu/ article/2012/10/24/presidential-candidates-image-may-trump-debate -issues.

Hunter, Mark Lee. *Story-Based Inquiry: A Manual for Investigative Journalists.* Paris: UNESCO, 2011.

Lariscy, Ruthann. "Why Negative Political Ads Work." *CNN,* January 2, 2012. http://www.cnn.com/2012/01/02/opinion/lariscy-negative-ads.

McCarthy, Justin. "Trust in Mass Media Returns to an All-Time Low." *Gallup.* September 17, 2014. http://www.gallup.com/poll/176042/trust-mass -media-returns-time-low.aspx

Moore, Martha T. "Bipartisan Commission Urges Early Voting, Shorter Lines." *USA Today,* January 22, 2014. http://www.usatoday.com/story/news /politics/2014/01/22/obama-election-commission/4771601.

Skewes, Elizabeth A. *Message Control: How News Is Made on the Presidential Campaign Trail.* Plymouth, UK: Rowman & Littlefield, 2007.

"Understanding Bias." *American Press Institute.* Accessed February 1, 2015. http://www.americanpressinstitute.org/journalism-essentials/bias -objectivity/understanding-bias.

Wagner, Kurt. "Midterm Elections Are More Social Than Ever." *Recode,* November 3, 2014. http://recode.net/2014/11/03/pew-study-midterm -elections-are-more-social-than-ever.

Waldman, Paul. "Mega-Blitz of Ad Spending Makes It Easier for Candidates to Lie." *Washington Post,* October 16, 2014. http://www.washingtonpost .com/blogs/plum-line/wp/2014/10/16/mega-blitz-of-ad-spending-makes -it-easier-for-candidates-to-lie.

FURTHER INFORMATION

Donovan, Sandy. *Special Interests: From Lobbyists to Campaign Funding.* Minneapolis: Lerner Publications, 2016. Read more about how special interest groups and political parties work with the media to influence elections.

Dziedzic, Nancy G. *Election Spending.* Detroit: Greenhaven, 2012. Learn about the relationship between the media and election spending from this collection of articles.

Elections—Congress for Kids
http://www.congressforkids.net/Elections_index.htm
Learn more about candidates, political parties, and elections in this interactive site just for kids.

McPherson, Stephanie Sammartino. *Political Parties: From Nominations to Victory Celebrations.* Minneapolis: Lerner Publications, 2016. Learn about how political parties influence elections.

Miller, Debra A., ed. *Federal Elections.* Detroit: Greenhaven, 2010. Learn directly from primary sources in this collection of articles about elections.

Presidential Campaign and Election Kit for Kids—Our White House
http://www.ourwhitehouse.org/campaignandelectionkit.html
Find information, resources, and activities to dig deeper into the topic of presidential elections.

PHOTO ACKNOWLEDGMENTS

The images in this book are used with the permission of: © iStockphoto.
com/cajoer, (banners); © iStockphoto.com/jamtoons, (arrows),
(stars), (speech bubbles); © iStockphoto.com/ginosphotos, (bunting);
© iStockphoto.com/Kontrec, (chalkboard); © iStockphoto.com/
OliaFedorovsky, (lines); © Chip Somodevilla/Getty Images, p. 5; AP Photo/
Kathy Willens, p. 7; © Andrew Harrer/Bloomberg/Getty Images, p. 11;
© Peter Macdiarmid/Getty Images for Meet the Press, p. 18; © iStockphoto.
com/Jacob Ammentorp Lund, p. 26; © Don Emmert/AFP/Getty Images, p. 29;
AP Photo/Manuel Balce Ceneta, p. 31; AP Photo/Star Tribune, Elizabeth
Flores, p. 32; © Robert Duyos/Sun Sentinel/MCT/Getty Images, p. 36; © Jake
Chessum/The Life Premium Collection/Getty Images, p. 37; © Kristoffer
Tripplaar/Alamy, p. 41 (right); © Marvin Dembinsky Photo Associates/
Alamy, p. 41 (left); © Apples Eyes Studio/Shutterstock.com, p. 46; © Karen
Bleier/AFP/Getty Images, p. 52; © Scott Barbour/Getty Images, p. 54.

Front cover: © iStockphoto.com/Kontrec (chalkboard background);
© iStockphoto.com/Electric_Crayon (border); © iStockphoto.com/StasKhom
(people and capitol); © iStockphoto.com/cajoer (banners); © iStockphoto.
com/OliaFedorovsky (patterns); © iStockphoto.com/jamtoons
(doodle arrows).

Back cover: © iStockphoto.com/jamtoons (doodle arrows) (stars).